Giraffes

by Grace Hansen

Abdo
SUPER SPECIES
Kids

abdopublishing.com

Published by Abdo Kids, a division of ABDO, PO Box 398166, Minneapolis, Minnesota 55439.

Copyright © 2017 by Abdo Consulting Group, Inc. International copyrights reserved in all countries. No part of this book may be reproduced in any form without written permission from the publisher.

Printed in the United States of America, North Mankato, Minnesota.

052016

092016

 THIS BOOK CONTAINS RECYCLED MATERIALS

Photo Credits: iStock, Minden Pictures, Shutterstock

Production Contributors: Teddy Borth, Jennie Forsberg, Grace Hansen

Design Contributors: Laura Mitchell, Dorothy Toth

Cataloging-in-Publication Data

Names: Hansen, Grace, author.

Title: Giraffes / by Grace Hansen.

Description: Minneapolis, MN : Abdo Kids, [2017] | Series: Super species |
     Includes bibliographical references and index.

Identifiers: LCCN 2015959212 | ISBN 9781680805444 (lib. bdg.) |
     ISBN 9781680806007 (ebook) | ISBN 9781680806564 (Read-to-me ebook)

Subjects: LCSH: Giraffe--Juvenile literature.

Classification: DDC 599.638--dc23

LC record available at http://lccn.loc.gov/2015959212

Table of Contents

Towering Mammal!

Giraffes are the tallest **mammals** on Earth. They can grow up to 20 feet (6 m) tall!

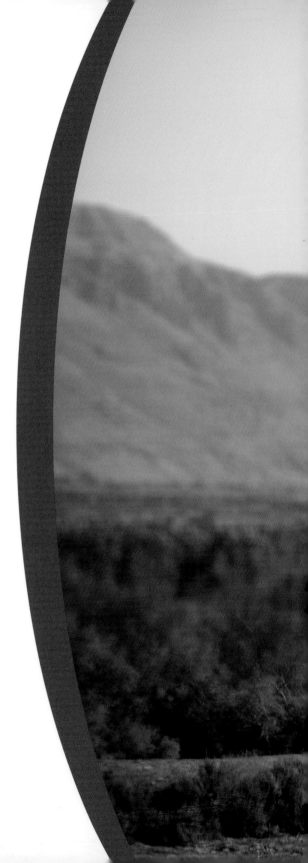

4

A giraffe's legs can be

a towering 6 feet (1.8 m) long.

That is taller than most humans.

6 ft

7

A giraffe's neck can

also be 6 feet (1.8 m) long.

The neck alone weighs up

to 600 pounds (272 kg)!

Giraffes use their height to their advantage. Their long legs help them run fast. They can reach speeds of 30 miles per hour (48 km/h).

Giraffes can also reach food that other animals cannot. They eat leaves high up in the treetops.

13

Some leaves are just out

of reach. Not to worry!

A giraffe's 20-inch (51-cm)

tongue can get those leaves.

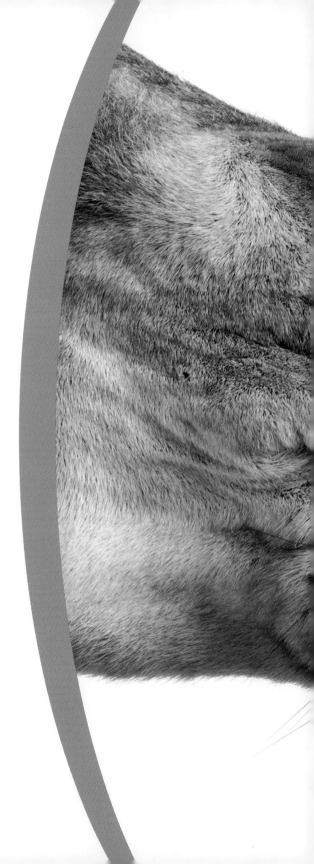

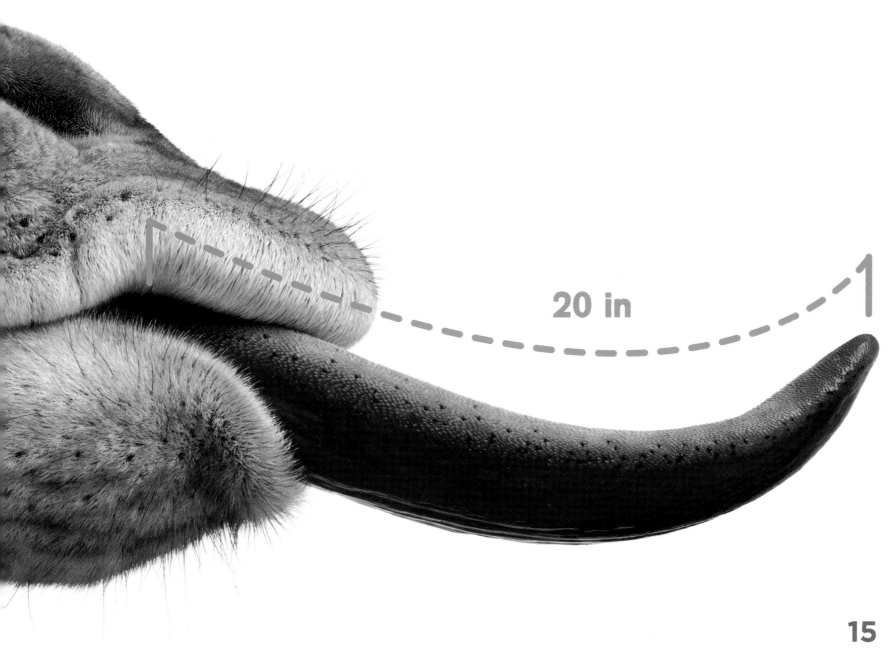

20 in

A giraffe gets lots of water from the leaves it eats. But sometimes it must drink from a watering hole. This can be **awkward** for the tall animal.

Hello World!

Newborn giraffes have quite the welcome into the world. Female giraffes give birth standing up. So babies fall at least 5 feet (1.5 m) to the ground.

Giraffes are already

6 feet (1.8 m) tall at birth!

Amazingly, babies stand

up 30 minutes after birth.

They can run soon after that.

More Facts

- A giraffe's tongue is used for more than eating. A giraffe uses its tongue to clean its ears and nose!

- Giraffes live in Africa. They mainly roam the grasslands.

- Giraffes can weigh up to 2,800 pounds (1,270 kg)!

22

Glossary

advantage – benefit or gain.

awkward – difficult and not graceful.

mammal – a type of animal that feeds milk to its young and that usually has hair or fur covering most of its skin.

23

Index

abdokids.com

Use this code to log on to abdokids.com and access crafts, games, videos, and more!

Abdo Kids Code:
SGK5444